I'M NOT PLAYING

ERICA LOBERG

chipmunkapublishing
the mental health publisher

ERICA LOBERG

All rights reserved, no part of this publication may be reproduced by any means, electronic, mechanical photocopying, documentary, film or in any other format without prior written permission of the publisher.

>Published by
>Chipmunkapublishing
>United Kingdom

http://www.chipmunkapublishing.com

Copyright © 2020 **ERICA LOBERG**

ISBN   978-1-78382-5332

I'M NOT PLAYING

Dedicated to all those that rise above
the ashes

in life.

ERICA LOBERG

ERICA LOBERG

Sometimes you get kicked
in the face.

Your cat eats the plant you've been growing for years
right in front of you.

You realize you're not always going to get the outcome
that you deserve.

Sometimes you start your engine
and the battery is dead.

Sometimes you are so beaten-down
that you look at yourself and say,

Wow.

How did I make it through
the hardships?

The hits
on my soul?

And walk out
someone else?

Not a broken person
but a new refreshed being.

I walk out...

Erica Loberg

ERICA LOBERG

ASHES

Ashes
Ashes

We all fall down.

My Father used to say,

*Little girls should be seen
and not heard.*

I should be seen
and heard.

Ashes
Ashes

We all fall down.

Commentary: When my Dad died no one in my family knew what to with his remains. Death wasn't something our family ever discussed. We decided to cremate him, but we never decided as a family what we should do with his ashes. When they were delivered to the house, in a plastic bag inside a cardboard box, they were left on the living room table. They sat beside his UCLA Facility of the Year Award. By the time they had arrived at the house, our family was taken over, and the ashes just sat there. Sitting. Waiting. While things fell apart.

I'M NOT PLAYING

ALLL ALONG THE WAYYY

Lawyers have one goal.

Spend someone else's money spend someone else's money
Spend someone else's money.

Then delay delay delay.

Then I can spend someone else's money spend someone else's money
Spend someone else's money.

So in effect, I can

Take all their money.

Cause the more I delay
The more I can charge so
The more I can get.

While I
Spend someone else's money spend someone else's money
Spend someone else's money.

That I'll get
By delaying
And take it

Allll along the wayyy.

Commentary: It didn't take me long to discover that my Mother's conservator's lawyers were spearheading his network of corruption. They would show up to court and flat-out lie. They would say they had not received pertinent documents needed to discuss the case, which would result in ongoing delays. I didn't know you could lie under oath but apparently you can. This happened on more than one occasion that it got to the point where I was like WTF? That is all they do. They show up, find a way to delay the case, so they can continue to spend more of my Mother's money. It was ridiculous. You want to play like that? Cause I'm not playing.

GUESTS OF GUESTS MAY NOT BRING GUESTS

"Guests of guests may not bring guests."

It's a sign my family
got for Christmas
after Thanksgiving,

One year.

I called my cousin and asked,

Are they talking about you, or about me?

She didn't know.
I didn't know.

We both received a sign from my Uncle and Aunt saying,

"Guests of guests may not bring guests."

Commentary: When my cousin and I talked about the sign, we were like, did you bring a bad boyfriend, or someone you shouldn't have to Thanksgiving? Did something happen cause we were too shitfaced to know any better? Did someone eat turkey out of the garage when they tried to hide the leftovers? We both didn't know who the sign was for, or what it was referring to, but my family got the sign wrapped up as a present for Christmas. I'll take ownership of it. Even if I don't know the guest that I brought that should not be a guest that may not bring guests.

THE JOKER AND BATMAN

I'll come at you from the left
I'll come at you from the right
I'll come at you standing up
I'll come at you sitting down
I'll come at you in the morning
I'll come at you at night.

You won't see me coming.

Cause I am an unstoppable force.

You're just an immovable object.

Commentary: In the final scene from, "Batman The Dark Knight," the Joker says to Batman, "You just couldn't let me go, could you? This is what happens when an unstoppable force meets an immovable object." One night I was watching the movie, and I realized I was dealing with a sociopath. The Joker was my Mother's conservator, and I was Batman. All I had to do was keep coming at him, hit him at every possible angle, and not give up. When I started to come across families at the mercy of this sociopathic Joker, they couldn't seem to stop him. Some of them would simply give up. They would either run out of money trying to fight him, or lack the energy to remove him, but I couldn't let him go. I was facing him alone with an unstoppable persistence, and I didn't spend a dime.

THE AWNING

I stare out my window and think maybe tonight I'll go out
It has been awhile and it's Saturday night.

In Downtown life doesn't open till late and I go to bed at 8
I look down to the street at a local bar.

I see a homeless person leaning outside against the
barricade of the bar
Beneath an awning.

It's raining.

If I decide to go out and enter that bar
I'll check out the awning.

I'll see how much it protects people
From the rain.

Cause they're going to protect the customers
Smoking cigarettes outside near the rain later tonight.

Tomorrow
Another homeless person will need shelter.

From something.

Commentary: I have these sweet binoculars that my Dad gave me as a housewarming gift when I moved into my loft in DTLA. Some nights I find myself taking them out and checking out what's going on in my neighborhood. I wrote this poem at a time in my life when I was isolating a lot. I didn't have much of a nightlife, but observing people on the street would give me some form of human contact. Even if it wasn't tangible, the fact I can reflect and write about my observations through poetry allowed me the chance to have a bridge between humankind versus being a total recluse. Thanks for the binoculars Dad, and thanks to poetry for your extended hand.

I FEEL BAD FOR THE CAT

Mom...

I'm really struggling right now.
All I have is my cat.
I just keep petting him.
I said.

I feel bad for the cat.
She said.

Commentary: My Mom's one-liners. Classic.

FLYYYY

I pump the pen

turn a page

I'm back.

Give me a pen
a purpose and I'll

Flyyyy.

Commentary: I have this funny-looking pen that I got from work. It's from the Department of Mental Health and has this head on the top with wild green hair. Green the color for mental health awareness, and wild hair to signify life with a mental illness? On the side it says LAC/DMH 24/7 ACCESS line 1-800-854-7771. It's ironic that the pen to bring me back to writing has a hotline for those that need emergency mental health services.

SNIVELING

I have a friend that reminds me of my Dad
We went out once and I used the term, "sniveling."

He had never heard that term before

He loved it.

Sniveling.

When my Dad used to take

My sisters and I on
Tortuous 5-mile hikes

When we were only 8 years old
Our feet would hurt.

We would complain

And he'd say,

Quit your sniveling!

Commentary: I miss my Father. He died 11 days after being diagnosed with cancer at the age of sixty-nine, but I keep his sayings alive.

RESISTANCE

My friend said the path of resistance
should be the one that we take.

I haven't been writing that much
for too long of a time.

I have to wonder
why the resistance?

Is it cause it's about my dysfunctional family?
Does my resistance mean,

I'm dysfunctional?

EXCUSES

How many excuses are you going to
Live with?

How many excuses are you going to
Die with?

How many excuses are you going to
Make?

Commentary: We all make excuses to take action when we are met with challenges in life. I heard when you say something out loud it's more likely that it will occur. If you write something down, and it is in print, then that must *really* mean it will happen. I guess there's no turning back now. I thought of this poem when I was in the kitchen cooking carne asada, and raced to my desk to write it down. Then I made a promise to myself, I will write this book. I will run out of excuses. Enough is enough. Are you a writer, or not?

I'M NOT PLAYING

THE PREDATOR

May I speak with the social worker?

The nurse opened my Mother's chart
and gave me her number.

You know my Mother's conserved right?

The social worker said the paperwork was not
in the chart so
she couldn't share any information
with me.

I'm her daughter.

The anger mixed with disbelief simmered
in my mouth
and hurt the blood
in my veins.

Then she asked me his name…

J.S.
I said.

The loud silence on the other end of the line
Froze my boiling blood.

Do you know him?
Wait for it…

Yes. I worked in nursing homes several years ago, and he would prey on rich vulnerable white women.

Commentary: When my Mom was hospitalized, her conservator didn't alert me. When I found out a day later from my sibling, she was already being discharged. I sent her conservator an email saying it was unacceptable to hospitalize my Mom and not inform me. No reply. No surprises there, but when I contacted St. John's Hospital in Santa Monica to find out what was going on, this *random* social worker knew of my Mother's conservator as a self-serving predator, and he was *still* on the loose?

I'M NOT PLAYING

NOT TODAY, NOT TOMORROW, NOT EVER

Why are you shocked?

Is that the feeling
cause it's such madness?

Are you supposed to know
how you feel?

When you're in deep
with a toxic person?

I tried to block you
you call me from an unidentified number.

I try to ignore you
you show up at my door.

Over and
               over and
                             over again.

You're not going to lose
yourself
again.

You're not going to be
gas lite
again.

You're going to be the woman that sits inside you
ready to be
ready to fight
ready to continue to do great things.

Or else that dipshit wins
But...

Not today, not tomorrow, not ever.

ERICA LOBERG

Commentary: When I finally broke away from my ex he couldn't seem to let me go, and I was stuck in this horrible game. Days, months, maybe even years could have continued to go by with this nonsense. Block, unblock, ghost, troll, reappear, disappear, gaslight, manipulate, seduce, charm. I see right through your shit dipshit. I spent a lot of Saturday mornings in therapy instead of dance class, but eventually I was done playing games.

I'M NOT PLAYING

I FILED

I filed a report with Adult Protective Services, twice.

I filed a report with the California State Fiduciary Bureau, twice.

I filed a report with the Los Angeles Police Department, twice.

I filed a report with the Los Angeles County District Attorney's Office, twice.

I filed a report with the DA's County of LA Consumer Protection Division.

I filed a report with the DA's County of LA Bureau of Investigation.

I filed a report with the Consumer Financial Protection Bureau.

I filed a report with the Los Angeles Real Estate Fraud Unit.

I filed a report with the Los Angeles County Probate Investigator's Office.

I filed a report with the Los Angeles County Financial Fraud Unit.

I filed a report with the Attorney General's Bureau of Elderly Abuse.

I filed a report with the California Department of Aging Advocacy Program.

I filed a report with California State Health Advocates.

I filed a report with the Dept. of Managed Care/Office Patient Advocate.

I filed a report with the U.S. Senate Special Committee on Aging.

I filed a report with the Federal Bureau of Investigation.

I FILED REPORTSSSSSSSSSSSSSSSSSSS.

Commentary: The two most vulnerable populations in the world are children and the elderly. By definition, a conservatorship is a court case where a judge appoints a *responsible person* or organization (called the "conservator") to care for another adult (called the "conservatee") who cannot care for himself or herself or manage his or her own finances. *That* is total malarkey. I don't understand why we have a system of checks and balances in place to protect children, while old people get abused and taken advantage of just to rot away. It blows my mind how the levels of corruption in the treatment of conservatees exist. When it happened to my Mom, I reached out to every entity that should be able to help me. I would get rejection letters after denial letters after return to sender letters. It became clear to me that I was going to have to do this on my own. When I stormed the streets to the Probate Human Resources Department at Superior Court to research my Mother's conservator, I stood in the hallway at one of the computers. I typed in his name, and there it was. Case number after case number after case number appeared on the screen. I took pictures of all the pages and walked home. I didn't know where to start, but I had to start somewhere. I went through the objectors on all of the cases. I knew that someday all this would come out, and no one can say that no one told them. Document, document, document. That was the name of the game.

THE HONOR

Does anyone have something else to say, or add?

The Honor asked.

My mind scrabbled with my heart

Fear mixed with uncertainty

Smothered my confidence.

I stood silent.

It only took that one time to learn my lesson.

I used to be afraid of judges in Superior Court
But not anymore.

I'd like my Dad's Rancho Relaxo neon sign back, and his ashes.

Commentary: I remember when my Mother was first conserved, toward the end of the hearing the judge asked if anyone had anything to add. I wanted to say something, but was afraid. After multiple court hearings in an effort to remove my Mothers conservator I was able to successfully remove him, but that was only after he stole everything from our house. Everything: furniture, paintings, china, clothes, jewellery, and the list goes on and on till there was nothing left. Although I didn't speak up in the first hearing, it doesn't change the fact that to this day, I don't know where my Dad's ashes are, and want that damn tacky neon Rancho Relaxo sign back. At least I got my Mom back, and freed her from a criminal.

BACHELOR NATION

I can see myself spending the rest of my life with him.
After two weeks.

I can see myself spending a night in the fantasy suite with her.
After two nights.

They sit around
on a beach
all day
half naked
searching to
be alive
with, "the one."

Another half.

He cries.
She cries.

It's love blowing up people in a house
or on an island.

Like, "Lord of the Flies."

Commentary: I'll never understand Bachelor Nation, but even worse, why *sometimes* I partake in it.

UPRISING

Hello Universe, Goodbye Universe!

People around the world

pray
       beg
              plead
                      wish
                             wait
                                      hope

For a sign from the universe.

Especially when things are bad.

If someone is struggling
or lost
or confused
or lonely
or afraid
or whatever.

The universe speaks to me
All the time
And I say,

Hello universe, goodbye universe!

Commentary: After my Father died, I decided I was going to write a book about grieving, and family trauma, about a lot of stuff. I received all these signs from the universe to buckle down and write, but for whatever reason, I chose to ignore the signs. Looking back, I am filled with regret, however, maybe I wasn't in a place to sit down and write at the time. Grieving is a tricky thing. Now the universe has given up on providing me guidance, but lesson learned. I know once I pick up the pen the universe will guide me. It may be pissed at me, so I owe it something.

THE REASSIGNMENT

It's like getting a pink slip under your door
But it's electronic over your desktop.

You have been reassigned.

Report at this date, this time, this place
Blah, blah, blah.

What the heck has life brought me?

The reassignment.

Commentary: I was not shocked when I got the email with the reassignment notice; I was a lot of things. I had worked as a family advocate for the mentally ill for over three years, and our unit was getting dismantled. A bunch of disgruntled people had filed grievances and now, we all had to take a hit. I had a previous co-worker that had an ongoing joke about how Los Angeles County would handle their employees. He would say, "Just like that." You literally get moved out of nowhere, transported, transferred, and dropped into somewhere foreign, out of nowhere just like that. I guess I'm just an item on some spreadsheet in Human Resources.

RUNNING LINES

Ok, I can do this…

Run drop turn
Run drop turn
Run drop turn
Run drop turn
Run drop turn
Run drop turn
Run drop turn
Run drop turn

Andddd puke.

Commentary: My Doctor put me on high blood pressure medication which upset me cause, I work out, and I'm not *that* old. I'm not fat just not my usual comfortable weight. Quite frankly, you can't be a white girl from the Westside and *not* be underweight. I guess the elliptical is a joke, and weights aren't doing much for me either. Obviously, I was not getting my heart rate up, so when I decided to run lines at the John Wooden basketball court at the Los Angeles Athletic Club for the first time since college, I got sick. Thankfully I had an empty stomach, and had only downed some Gatorade prior to working out, so that's all that came up. Looks like I'll be running lines again cause whatever workout routine I was doing was not working out. Literally.

A CROSS

I looked up at the ceiling
There it was

A cross.

It stared down at me
I thought

That's weird.

I've been trying to meditate on and off for years
Usually I'd do the rosary in the steam room
But now I use it to suck cold water out of an ice cube bag.

When I found the quiet room
In the locker room

I tried to meditate
I tried to find myself with God.

But I didn't expect to look up and see,

A cross.

Commentary: I have always tried to connect with God, and myself, and this was the first day I had tried in several years. It just so happened that on that first day in the quiet room in the gym - lying down staring up at the ceiling - there it was. It wasn't an actual traditional cross. The ceiling was made with giant tiles with crosses on them. This tile was directly above my bed with what looked like a cross. Was this a sign? I thought to myself was this the shift I needed to find that person deep inside that was the true me, the me that loved me, and would now rise up?

YE OLDE KING'S HEAD aka THE GOOD OLD COLLEGE TRY

The night before Thanksgiving was always worth
A good old college try.

My Dad and whoever was up for it
Would go to a pub in Santa Monica and play darts.

At Ye Olde King's Head.

One year I didn't go
I was living in West Hollywood at the time
I got up early and arrived at the house in Westwood

Ready to go.

I walked into the house
It was a quiet crime scene.

Someone was passed out on the living room sofa
Someone was in the kitchen slowly getting water out of the fridge dispenser.

I heard my Dad from the top of the stairs
We'll be ready in ten minutes.

Hurting hangover central.

We'd all get in the car
Drive up North to Thanksgiving

Someone puked in their shoe that year
On the way in the car.

Ye Olde King's Head
For a good old college try!

THE BONDS GUY

Discreet doesn't begin to cover it
Looming
Weird
Shady
Discreet

Almost like working behind the scenes.

Which you were
Which you are
Which you will continue…

Your game won't last much longer.

Commentary: Once I started to take a good look around the courthouse, and pick up on who the players were in this scam, I noticed this guy that would come in late to hearings and sit in the corner in the back. He was a shadow of compliance from," Bond Services of California." I chased him down one time in the hallways after one of the hearings, and asked him for his card. I called him later that day and said, "You know J.S. is a criminal right?" He was quiet for longer than a usual response then replied, "I'm not sure what you are talking about. "Ok, I see how it is," and I hung up. He was on J.S.'s team. Did I have concrete proof? No, my instincts were enough.

WELCOME BACK NOTEPAD

She's back
it's back.

My notepad.

I lie in bed
my mind scrambles.

Ideas sprout out
like a saltshaker.

It's dark so I flip open my laptop
to use the computer screen for a light.

Scribble.
Scribble.
Scribble.

The light is dim
I hope I can read it tomorrow.

She's back.

ERICA LOBERG

EVERY SHAMING STEP OF THE WAY

I'm not sure when it started but
it goes way back to about 5 years old.

Erica, you're too sensitive!

I was shamed
a lot.

It seeps in periodically
throughout your life.

It shapes you into someone
that you're not.

You carry insecurities
and you don't know why.

You question your decisions
and you don't know why.

Your inability to find your inner child
gets buried.

Every shaming step of the way
but it's not forever.

Once you listen you hear that self
it will slowly start to grow.

It will nurture your spirit
that thrives in sorrow, conquers in uncertainties, rises to challenges.

It will become a source of power
to overcome that shame.

Then you realize the source
of that shame

Is not yours

I'M NOT PLAYING

so

Shame on me,
no.

Shame on you,
for shaming me!

Commentary: It took me years to begin to understand why parts of me are the way that they are due to being shamed as a child. The good thing is, no matter what your age, you can develop a better understanding of your authentic self, and that self will be waiting right there for you. That person will not let you down. The door is always open if you decide to do the work it takes to crawl through it. Yeah, I'd start by thinking of it as *crawling*.

ERICA LOBERG

BLACK PANTHER AND ROBIN

I wasn't supposed to be exposed to the sun
But by the time I got home on my Vespa
The damage was already done.

I sat and watched, "The View" on my lap top
Waiting
There was an interview with the actor from the movie, "Black Panther."

2 pm
Right on time

There was a knock at my door.

I opened it to an agent and said,
I hope you are my new Black Panther.

Than another agent stepped forward,
And you must be Robin.

They came in and sat down.

I offered them Cadbury chocolate eggs on a plate
With two fresh glasses of water
And said,

Please ignore my face, I don't have leprosy, just some skin cancer issues.

Commentary: When I met with the FBI to give them all the evidence I had on the Villain, I had a skin treatment the day before. I wasn't supposed to be in the sun so when I got home my face was all red and blotchy. It was poor timing, but whatever. I handed over all the files that I had, and we spent a couple hours going over the case. I knew they wouldn't be able to share any other information with me while conducting the investigation. As time went on I just kept sending them leads with no idea where things stood on their end. Then one night I got frustrated and sent an email to Black Panther stating, "Well, I guess I'm just going to have to keep taking it up the ass till justice is serviced." Yeah, *that* happened.

ERICA LOBERG

HEARING BEFORE YOU CAN LISTEN

When I look back at some of my writing
It's always a reflection of my journey.

Some of it is angry, but real
Provocative, but honest
Intense, but transparent.

I take pride in the honesty of my work
I scream at the top of my lungs to get people
To hear.

To learn, to see, to feel, to experience
Honesty.

You have to hear before you can listen.

It's not that I am going to sell out
Or change my style or point of view.

But poetry is a reflection of
Wherever you are in life
Whoever you are at the time.

As long as I keep trying
To make people hear

Eventually

They will listen.

Commentary: As I evolve as a human being, I do my best to stays true to my journey and to myself. Do I still have dark thoughts? Yes. Do I still get pissed off at and feel like it's me against the world? Yes. There are also other sides of the self that can be explored through the written word, so I'll keep it moving.

I'M NOT PLAYING

TRAUMA

Trauma.

It can sit in the heart
of your soul.

Someone puts their hand on your shoulder
you jump.

And you don't know why.

You can lack confidence and question
your every move.

And you don't know why.

You can wake up in a deep sweat
catching the end of a nightmare.

And you don't know why.

But when it bubbles to the surface
and releases itself
from the heart of the soul
you begin to wonder...

How long have I not known why?

Commentary: When something traumatic occurs, sometimes we don't always know that it's happening, or know how to process it. Our being can go into shock and it gets buried in the back of the mind. Then days, months, or years can go by, and it manifests itself. You might not be able to pin point the source, but it's there. It was always there.

ERICA LOBERG

SKID ROW

People don't want to talk about it
People don't want to look at it
People don't want to be near it
People don't want to smell it
People don't want to read about it
People don't want to know about it
People don't want to walk around rats
People don't want to get scabies
People don't want to be exposed to tuberculosis
People don't want to acquire a flesh eating disease
People don't want to get lice
People don't want to be surrounded by tents
People don't want to see a broken human race

People don't know what to do about it

Skid Row.

Commentary: Homelessness is beyond a crisis, or an epidemic, it's apocalyptic. What frustrates me is people throw money at the situation without knowing the problem. I used to do homeless outreach and would walk the streets of Skid Row. When I would meet with the Board of Supervisors of LA County to discuss the issues, it was in *their* offices. It was air conditioned with clean carpets, and dust free tabletops. I had to sit across the table with some suit that had a beautiful view of LA County, and had never stepped foot on homeless grounds.

ORDER TO SHOW CAUSE

I was sitting at my desk when the email came in
I opened the doc and started to bleed.

Erica is only after her Mother's money
Erica has emotional issues
Erica should be restricted from speaking to her Mother.

The allegations were horrific and went on and on and on.

I put it away and thought, ok, I'll deal with this next week
I don't need a meltdown at work.

Not today.

Commentary: Once my Mother's conservator realized I was after him, he tried to put a restraining order on me to keep me from talking to my Mom. He tried to make an argument that I was causing my Mom stress by voicing my concerns about him stealing all her money. Well, yeah, she should be upset. Someone needs to tell her the truth. His slimy move was only going to blow up in his face cause I started to see a pattern of how he conducted his business. Isolate his victims, get restraining orders on family members that object to him, and keep taking everything. Once I found other victims, I would explain his plan of attack. Some of them listened. Others, not so much. After all, I was just a County employee that wrote poetry.

NOW

I've loved you for a long time, now.

When he said it I wasn't sure what he meant
We had been friends for several years
Did he mean he loved me as a friend, or more than a friend?

When I break down the sentence, and think about the word, "now"
I think it means more than a friend
As if his feelings have been growing for a long time

Now.

Am I reading into one word too much, now?

Commentary: I became quiet after my friend said that cause I wasn't sure how to respond. Since I didn't know how I felt about him, or exactly what he meant, I just let it go. After that night he kinda dropped out of my life. He stopped texting me and calling me and making plans to get together. He probably felt rejected since I didn't say anything and as time went on, it became hard to revisit that comment. I've always paid close attention to diction in language. I should have just given him this poem if I wasn't capable of having a conversation about it.

> In the truly great poets, there is a reason assignable, not only for every word, but for the position of every word.
> (Samuel Taylor Coleridge.)

I'M NOT PLAYING

SIZZLE

My face felt like a red-hot flaming Cheeto.

I don't know how many times I was going
to burn the shit out of
my skin.

To remove the precancerous cells
that sprinkled all over
my face.

The dermatologist said I had the skin
of a 70-year-old
Caucasian male.

I don't know why she said male
when I'm a female but
maybe women take better care of their skin.

Not this sizzling moron!

Skiing, surfing, sailing, tennis, volleyball….

Burn that bitching skin

Sizzle, sizzle, sizzle.

Commentary: Growing up a fair-skinned redhead with freckles, I was ashamed of my skin. My peers would make fun of me in middle school, "Freckle face, freckle face, you are a freckle face!" My solution was to burn my skin to try and hide them. Now, I am paying the price for being insecure about my skin. "Cancer face, cancer face, you are a cancer face!"

SIMPLE ANSWER TO A SIMPLE QUESTION

Why don't you have children?

Cause I can't afford them.

Commentary: I get this question a lot. I always told myself that I would only have kids if I could afford them. Sometimes it's hard for me to see a bunch of kids hanging on the back of their Mom, and know that as a taxpayer it's possible that I am paying for some of those kids. I understand people need help at times, but if you can't afford one kid, you shouldn't have another one, or five.

THOSE EYES

You wear a moustache on your lip
Next.

You wear a beard on your chin
Next.

You change your clothes
Next.

You change your bag
Next.

You can change your face
You can change your clothes
You can't change

Those eyes.

Commentary: Every time I went to court and had to face my Mother's conservator, he had changed his appearance. One constant was his fixated eyes that looked like a sociopath. He always had this intense stare and would look straight ahead at the judge. Why not put some paint on your face like the Joker that you are while you're at it.

COMMONER

What are you, a lawyer?
No. I'm a commoner.

I'm going to hang up now.

Click.

Commentary: When I was researching victims of my Mother's conservator, I would contact any and all leads that I could find. In this particular situation, I was on the phone with a lawyer that was attached to one of the conservator's cases. When I started to discuss the criminal behavior of the conservator he cut me off. All he cared about was my title. Maybe I should have lied and said I was someone important. He might have stayed on the phone with me long enough to hear me out. Shakespeare said it best, "The first thing we do, let's kill all the lawyers." (Henry VI, Part 2, Act IV, Scene 2.)

I'M NOT PLAYING

You want to play?
Cause I'm not playing.

I pulled out every hit to my soul of their
Order to show cause case.

I tossed every defaming argument
Right back in their face.

You want to play?
Cause I'm not playing!

Commentary: When I received the paperwork from the lawyers for the order to show cause hearing, I copied their format, wrote my response, pounded the pavement to the Superior Court, and filed my own order to show cause. When I showed up to court to discuss *my* order to show cause, the judge said he hadn't seen it. That's ok. It felt good to at least try to shut down their ongoing attempts to take me down, despite that fact that no one ever read it.

ERICA LOBERG

I WAS JUST THE OFFICER OF THE DAY

I picked up the phone and heard tears from a soul
She was stuck in a nursing home
Alone, angry, afraid, suffering.

I was just the Officer of the Day.

I walked into a co-worker's office and said,
I don't understand why this is happening to me?

She turned around from her computer and said,
God chose you.

Commentary: It was wild. While I was working on bringing down my Mother's conservator, other victims were just falling out of the sky onto my lap. I worked as a family advocate and residents of LA County would contact our office for mental health related matters. This particular victim was removed from her home in Santa Monica, and shipped off to a nursing home in the valley. She was there against her will and was being held like a hostage. On this particular day, I walked into my co-worker's office to vent. When we first met I found out she had previously worked for the Public Guardians office of LA County, and she looked into my Mother's conservator and discovered he was impossible to remove. Not to mention the fact that I had evidence in an email from the Director of the Public Guardian's office concerning this particular victim. The email said she believed he had committed perjury in court, but they couldn't prove it. The conservator was able to get a psychiatrist to testify that this woman was delusional, so needed to be in an assisted living home. When I told my co-worker what was happening she said in all seriousness God chose me. I laughed and responded, "Oh, yes I am the anointed one." When I went back to my cube, I sat down and thought to myself, maybe she's right. Maybe there was a bigger reason for my circumstances. There was no other explanation for everything that was going down.

BLACK LIVES MATTER AND WHITE PEOPLE'S PROBLEMS

Black lives matter
Black lives matter, you know.

He breathed down my neck
while I waited in line at the Rite-Aid.

I just wanted to get my mosquito repellant and go home.

I stepped toward one of the cashiers,
Can you check me out?
I asked.

I'm not open.
He said.

Well, I'm being harassed.
I continued.

While everyone just stood there
watching.

You're going to need a black man to rescue you if there is a fire, you know.
He kept coming at me.

Do you want me to call someone?
The cashier asked.

I dropped the repellant
pissed off

And left.

Commentary: When I told one of my friends what had happened he said, "White people's problems." I didn't want to engage the harasser, but I'm not going to sit there and be accosted, so I left.

ERICA LOBERG

MACHIAVELLI

He stood in court
pasty and white.

He walked right by me
bald and sweaty.

His chest all pumped out
like a Minotaur.

At least in court
I didn't have to see his
lumpy
sandbag
tits.

It was Machiavelli.

Commentary: Machiavelli is the nickname I gave to the conservator's lawyer that I had to go up against in court on more than one occasion. He was also a member of my gym, and I would run into him from time to time when I was working out. When I started to research victims I spoke with families that knew him as a criminal just like the conservator, and his abuse of vulnerable elderly citizens of Los Angeles County went back two decades. Maybe my Dad was sending me messages, signs, and encouragement. I couldn't just accidentally keep running into him, and not be reminded of all the damage that he inflicted on victims. I got this, and whatever force was with me was carrying me under its wing.

FADING

I stood in front of the judge and started to cry.

My Mom is suffering.
My Mom is decompensating.
My Mom is isolated.
My Mom is slowly dying.

Fogarty's don't die, they fade.

I recalled my Mother telling me.

She was right.

Commentary: This marked the pivotal turning point of ridding my Mother of her conservator. I stood in front of the judge and argued a case that her mental, emotional, and psychological health was deteriorating. Often in these probate court hearings people focus on financial elderly abuse. Although that was occurring, I didn't go there cause his network of financial abuse was operating on a level beyond my control. I stuck to mental abuse. I told the truth, and it worked. I was able to temporarily remove him, and I walked home.

ERICA LOBERG

THE MEDIATION

We sat in an office in Century City
across the street from my Dad's old office building
where he used to practice his,

"Tooth Moving Company."

He said he would only step down
if we replaced him with one of his
suggestions
for another conservator.

I didn't know what to think
or do
or say
or not say.

I just wanted him out.

After a longgg ten hour day
we agreed to take his suggestion and...

He stepped down.

Commentary: After the mediation, I found out his "suggestion" used the same caregiver company that was part of his criminal network. I pounded the pavement to Superior Court in DTLA and filed paperwork to try and undo the outcome of the mediation. When I appeared in court the judge said he had not read the statement so I restated what I filed with the court. He heard me and scheduled another hearing to either confirm or deny my request. I was getting close, closer, the fight was still on and I was not giving up, with any gloves on.

THE LOS ANGELES TIMES

He was a Pulitzer Prize Journalist for the Los Angeles Times.

I wrote him
nothing.

I called him
something.

I pitched the story and told him
I would send him a list of victims.

The list was long with
names, numbers, and back stories.

Two years worth
of work.

Researching
Contacting people
Pounding pavements
Taking meetings with victims.

All I needed was a reputable voice to stamp their name on the expose.

I followed up…

I sent your information to the line staff.

What do you mean line staff?

It's not a big enough story for me.

Did you speak to any of the victims that I sent you?

Like I said, if the line staff is interested they'll contact you.

I knew he hadn't called any of the people on the list and exploded,

YOU'RE WRONGGG!

Commentary: Ok, I told a Pulitzer Prize winning journalist from the LA Times that he was wrong. I have zero regrets.

I'M NOT PLAYING

RUNNING LINES PART II

I'm doing this…

Run drop turn
Run drop turn
Run drop turn
Run drop turn
Run drop turn
Run drop turn
Run drop turn
Run drop turn
Run drop turn
Run drop turn
Run drop turn
Run drop turn
Run drop turn
Run drop turn
Run drop turn
Run drop turn
Run drop turn
Run drop turn
Run drop turn
Run drop turn
Run drop turn
Run drop turn
Run drop turn
Run drop turn

I'm back bitchessss!

THE PEN

I took out a pen that I received as a graduation present
from college.

It was a fancy Mont Blanc fountain pen
that had my initials engraved on the side.

I took out fancy paper to hand write
the letter.

I dipped the pen into the fresh ink
and wrote.

I told myself I would only use that pen
for something important.

I had waited twenty years
to use that pen.

Tonight was the night
to use it.

Commentary: When I lost the initial hearing and my Mom was appointed to her corrupt conservator, I had a gut feeling the court was somehow involved with his scam. When I showed up to the hearing I said, "This man is a criminal and belongs behind bars!" I attempted to present evidence of the victims and the judge immediately shut me down. I remember thinking something is not right here. Soon after the conservator was appointed, I decided to write the judge that had presided over the case a five page letter. I spelled out all the reasons why he was unfit as a conservator. I also questioned the court, wondering if they had something to do with it. Is everyone getting kickbacks, including the probate conservatorship department? Weeks later the letter was sent back to me along with the envelope that it was mailed in with a letter that stated they don't read any material having to do with the case. Yeah right: no letter, no evidence, no liability, and no accountability. I held onto the letter, and the return reply. Luckily, soon after my letter was sent back, that judge had retired, and we were appointed a new judge.

ERICA LOBERG

THE LETTER

Dear Judge Peterson,

My fancy pen ran out of ink so
I have to use
a regular one.

I'm writing to you cause you played a part in changing
the trajectory
of my Mother's life.

We had our final hearing today and
due to your ear throughout this mess
you were able to get Mother's criminal conservator removed.

I can't thank you enough
for the courage it takes
to listen.

Courage sounds like a funny word but
it takes courage and listening to do your job
which you did seamlessly with dignity and principle.

I can't thank you enough.

With respect and gratitude,

ERICA LOBERG

Commentary: *That* letter was never sent back.

www.ingramcontent.com/pod-product-compliance
Lightning Source LLC
Chambersburg PA
CBHW031216090426
42736CB00009B/943